on the wing

bird poems and paintings by

Douglas Florian

voyager books

harcourt, inc.

SAN DIEGO • NEW YORK • LONDON

First Voyager Books edition 2000
Voyager Books is a registered trademark of Harcourt, Inc.

The Library of Congress has cataloged the hardcover edition as follows:
Florian, Douglas.
On the wing/by Douglas Florian.
p.   cm.
Summary: A collection of poems about such birds as the
emperor penguin, rhinoceros hornbill, and whooping crane.
1. Children's poetry, American.   2. Birds—Juvenile poetry.
[1. Birds—Poetry. 2. American poetry.] I. Title.
PS3556.L58905 1996
811'.54—dc20   95-9976
ISBN 0-15-200497-1

ISBN 0-15-202366-6 pb

A C E F D B

PRINTED IN SINGAPORE

Contents

The Egret

On morning tide
An egret sat
And gave the beach
A feathered hat.

The Green Catbird

With feathers of a greenish hue
No doubt I'm difficult to view.
On vines and trees I'm inconspicuous.
They call me a cat—
Ain't *that*
Ridiculous.

The Dippers

Through splash and spray
Of waterfalls
Skip the little dippers.
I think that they
Would gladly trade
Their oily wings for flippers.
Inside a stream
They swim supreme,
For minutes if they wish—
These funny little songbirds
Who think that they are fish.

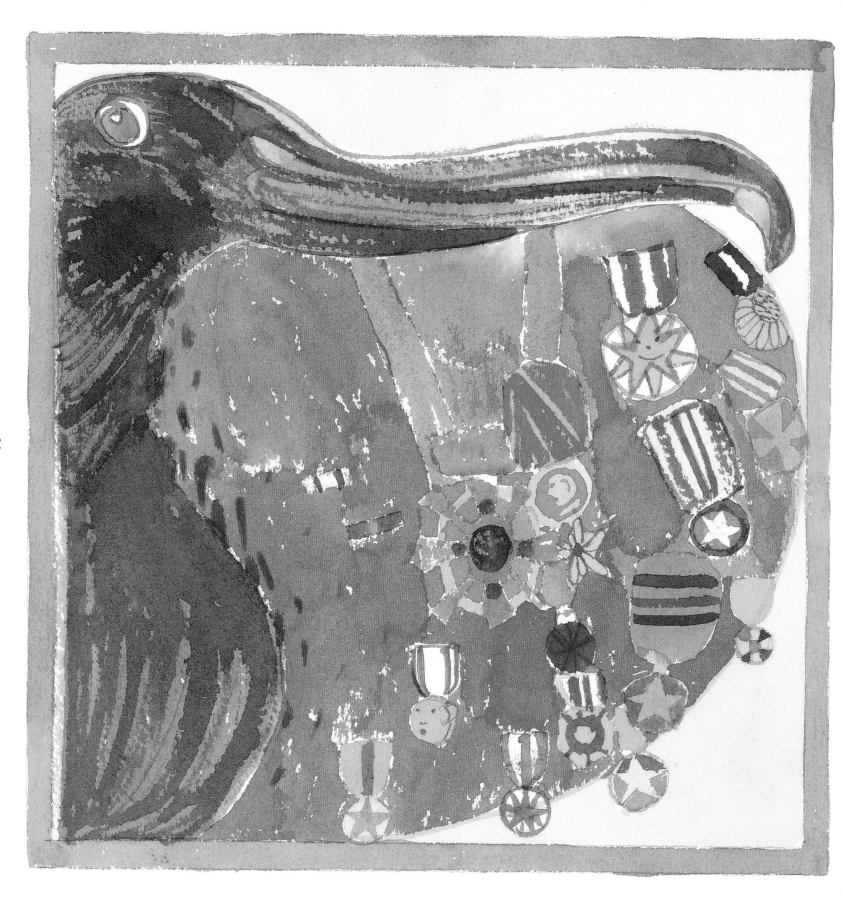

The Magnificent Frigate Birds

It's true,

      correct,

We do assent:

We really are

   MAGNIFICENT.

For endless hours

Serene we s o a r

Or g l i d e

Or w^h^{e}$_e$$_l$

And what is more

Our crimson chests

We can **inflate.**

How could you

NOT

Regard us great?

The Hummingbird

Barely bigger than your thumb,
See it hover, hear it hum,
With beating wings so fast they're blurred,
This *helicopter* of a bird.

The Vulture

Two things I know about the vulture:
Its beak
          is strong.
It's weak
          on culture.

The Whooping Crane

The whooping crane,
The whooping crane,
So big it's practically a plane.
A splendid sight
Up in the air—
It's lithe and light
But rather rare.
It feeds in marshes—
See it stoop—
This brilliant bird
That loves to whoop.

The Roadrunner

The roadrunner darts
Down dusty roads
In search of insects,
Lizards and toads.
Past tumbleweeds
It *speeds* for snakes,
And catching them,
Turns on the brakes.

The Quetzal

The

        fluorescent

           emerald

    getzal.   tail

    tail

              of

   bird

              the

    a

            quetzal

    as

          grows

      long

        as

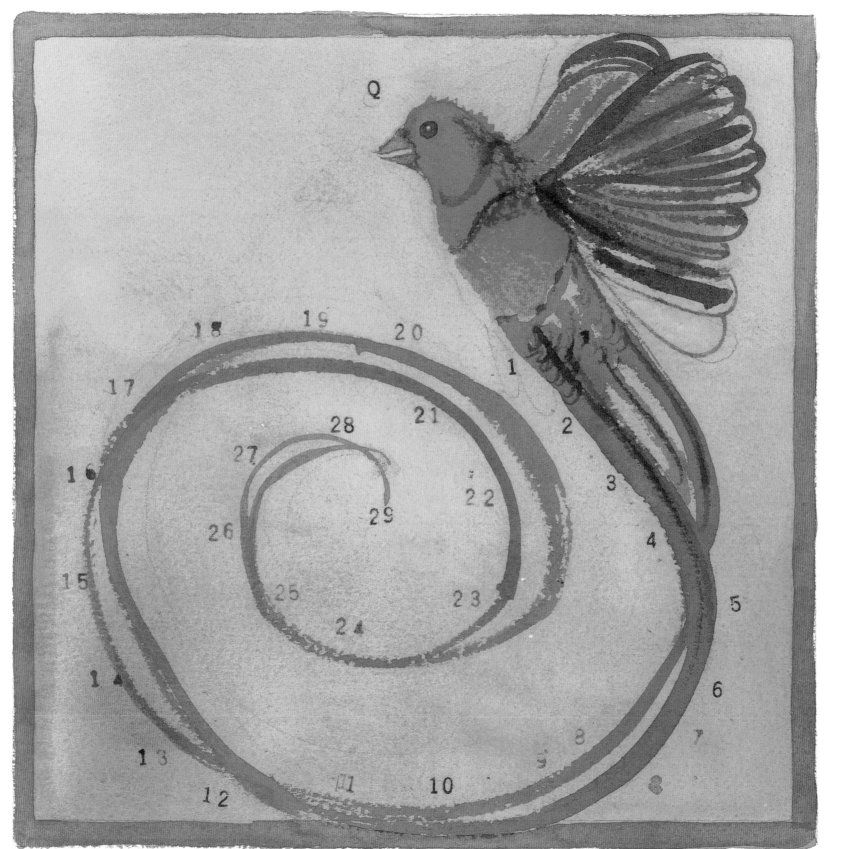

23

The Hill Mynah

I squawk
   I talk
      I even sing.
My voice can mimic anything.
In any tongue
I can converse.
I gab
   I blab
      I'm never terse.
I echo every word that's said.
(A tape recorder's in my head.)

The Royal Spoonbill

How fortunate and opportune
To have a nose that's like a spoon.
Did you descend from royalty,
And is your spoon for stirring tea?
Or do you use it as a scoop
For eating peas and drinking soup?

The Rhinoceros Hornbill

This Southeast Asian bird is born
With large and orange curving horn.
This massive growth is called a casque.
(For Halloween it needs no mask.)

The White-Tailed Kite

The wondrous white-tailed kite—
A never boring soaring sight
As it glides on gull-like wings,
A kite that flies but has no strings.

The Emperor Penguins

The life of these penguins
Is harsh as can be:
They gather on ice packs
Of antarctic sea,
All huddled together
For warmth and protection,
And choose a new emperor
Without an election.

The Hawk

I stare

      I glare

I gaze

      I gawk

With keen

Mean eyes

I am the hawk.

All day I pray

For prey to view.

Be thankful if

I don't

See

YOU!

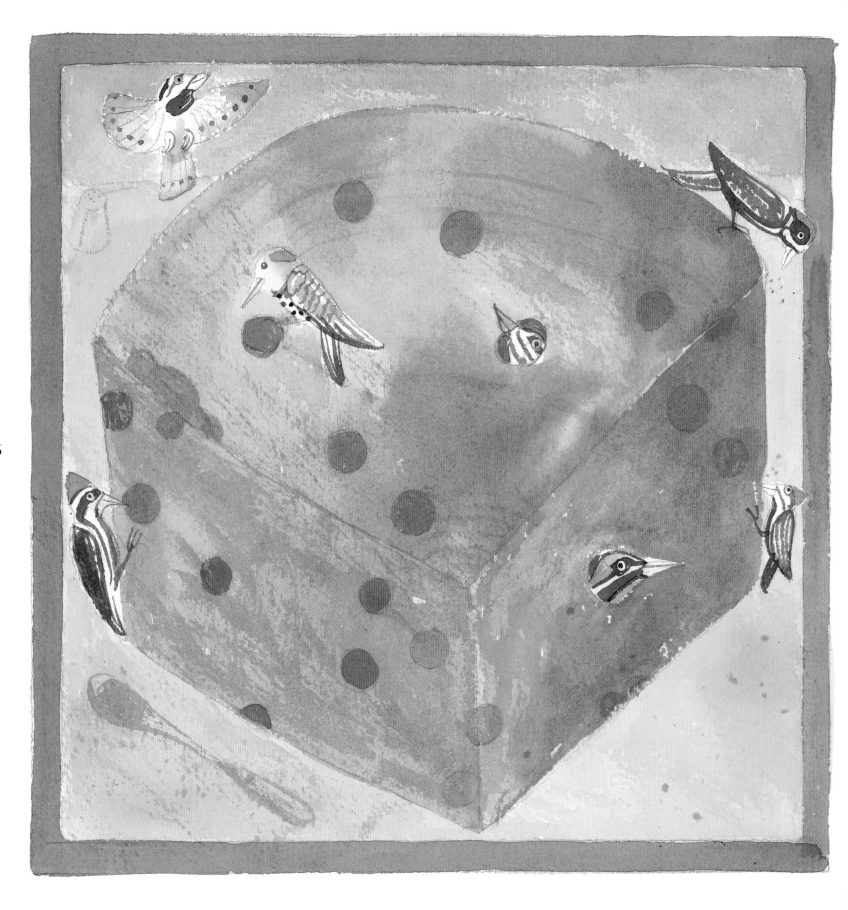

The Woodpeckers

Woodpeckers are *peckuliar* things.
They pick to peck but not to sing.
They rap
   and tap
      for sap in trees
Till some they drum
Look like Swiss cheese.
They thump on stumps of rotting wood
To gobble insects—
Mmmmmmmmmm, tastes good!

The Andean Cock-of-the-Rock

The Andean cock-of-the-rock
Has a crest that's as round as a clock.
   Its shoulders and head
   Are a flaming bright red—
Just to think of it gives me a shock.
Descending upon forest floor
It feeds upon fruit, and what's more,
   On ground or in trees,
   Each expert agrees,
This vivid bird can't be ignored.

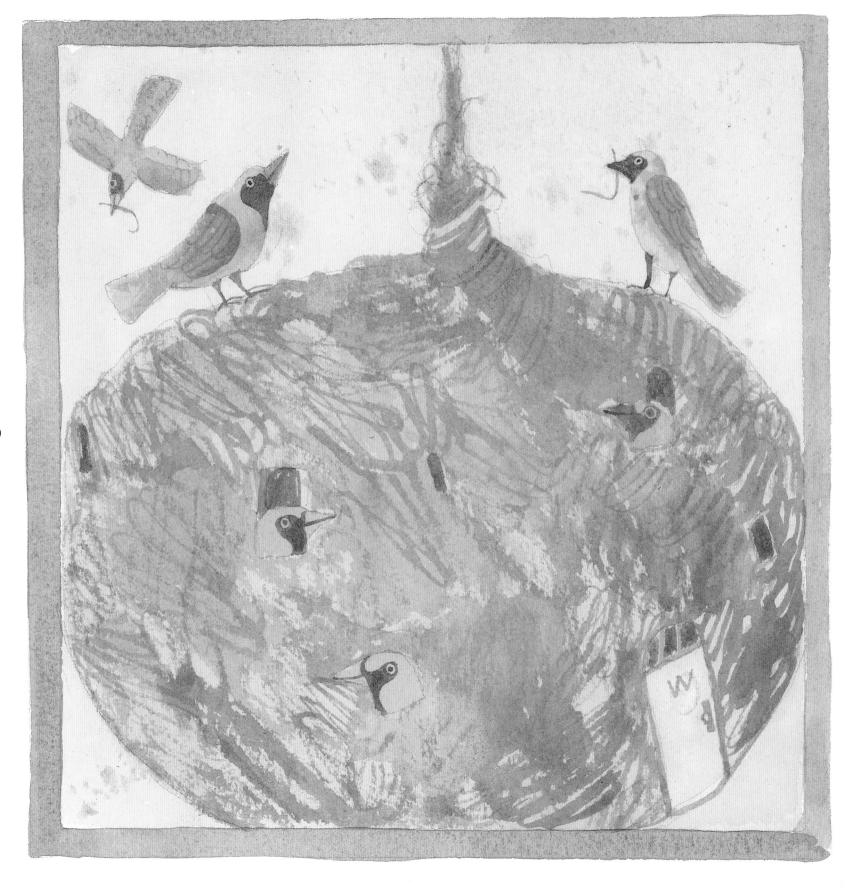

The Weavers

We are weavers—
Watch us weave
A spacious nest
From twigs and leaves,
Complete with walls
And roof
And floor—
When leaving please
Don't slam the door!

The Stork

Observe the large long-legged stork
With bill as sharp as knife or fork.
Its neck is curved.
Its wings are great.
It feeds on frogs without a plate.

44

The Common Crow

Frightening feet.
Likes to eat.
Harsh call.
Hardly small.
Black and glossy.
Rude and bossy.
Common crow.
Go! Go!

The Nightjar

By day this bird
Will stay at rest,
For darkness seems
To suit it best,
To chase down insects
Near and far,
And capture night
Inside a jar.